The grand essentials
to happiness
in this life are
something to do
something to love
and something
      to hope for.

Joseph Addison

Other books in the *"Language of"* Series... by

Blue Mountain Press ®

The Language of Love

The Language of Friendship

The Language of Marriage

The Language of Teaching

The Language of Courage and Inner Strength

Thoughts to Share with a Wonderful Mother

Thoughts to Share with a Wonderful Father

Thoughts to Share with a Wonderful Son

Thoughts to Share with a Wonderful Daughter

It's Great to Have a Brother like You

It's Great to Have a Sister like You

The Language of

HAPPINESS

A Collection from Blue Mountain Arts®

Edited by Susan Polis Schutz

Blue Mountain Press ®

Boulder, Colorado

Library of Congress Catalog Card Number: 98-42642
ISBN: 0-88396-480-5

ACKNOWLEDGMENTS appear on page 48.

Manufactured in Thailand
Third Printing: August 1999

♲ This book is printed on recycled paper.

Library of Congress Cataloging-in-Publication Data

The language of happiness / edited by Susan Polis Schutz.

    p.   cm.
    ISBN 0-88396-480-5 (alk. paper)
    1. Happiness--Quotations, maxims, etc. 2. Happiness--Poetry. I. Schutz, Susan Polis.
PN6084.H3L3 1999
170--dc21   98-42642

                                                                                          CIP

Blue Mountain Press INC.

P.O. Box 4549, Boulder, Colorado 80306

Contents

(Authors listed in order of first appearance)

Believe in What
Makes You Happy

Believe in what makes you feel good.
Believe in what makes you happy.
Believe in the dreams
    you've always wanted to come true,
      and give them every chance to.

Life holds no promises
    as to what will come your way.
You must search for your own ideals
    and work toward reaching them.
Life makes no guarantees
    as to what you'll have.
It just gives you time to make choices
    and to take chances
and to discover whatever secrets
    that might come your way.

If you are willing to take
    the opportunities you are given
        and utilize the abilities you have,
you will constantly fill your life
    with special moments
        and unforgettable times.

No one knows the mysteries of life
    or its ultimate meaning,
but for those who are willing
    to believe in their dreams
        and in themselves,
life is a precious gift
    in which anything is possible.

                                    Dena Dilaconi

Happiness...

Many persons have a wrong idea about what constitutes true happiness. It is not attained through self-gratification, but through fidelity to a worthy purpose.

 Helen Keller

Happiness cannot come from without. It must come from within. It is not what we see and touch or that which others do for us which makes us happy; it is that which we think and feel and do, first for the other fellow and then for ourselves.

Keep
your face to
    the sunshine
and you cannot
    see the shadow.

— Helen Keller

It's You That Makes Me Happy

To love is to place our happiness in the happiness of another.

> Gottfried Wilhelm von Leibnitz

I could not be what I am, if I did not take such serene happiness from my union with you. You are my spring of content; and so long as I have you, and you too are happy, nothing but good and power can come to me... may God bless and keep you!

> Woodrow Wilson

I sit here
bored
I don't feel like talking
to the people here
I don't feel like looking
at this place anymore

I sit here
lonely
realizing that it's not
people or places that
make me happy
It's you

 Susan Polis Schutz

It's You That Makes Me Happy

I wish you all the good and
charm that life can offer.
Think of me kindly, and…
rest assured that no one
would more rejoice to hear of
your happiness.

Love, and love alone,
is capable of giving
thee a happier life.

— Ludwig van Beethoven

Exuberance of Nature

Sounds of the wind
sounds of the sea
make one happy
just to be.

> — June Polis

Joy is everywhere;
it is in the earth's
green covering of grass:
in the blue
serenity of the sky:
in the reckless
exuberance of spring:
in the severe abstinence
of grey winter:
in the living flesh
that animates our bodily frame:
in the perfect poise
of the human figure,
noble and upright:
in living, in the exercise
of all our powers:
in the acquisition of knowledge
...Joy is there everywhere.

> — Rabindranath Tagore

☆ Philosophy of Happiness ☆

I have never given very deep thought to a philosophy of life, though I have a few ideas that I think are useful to me. One is that you do whatever comes your way to do as well as you can, and another is that you think as little as possible about yourself and as much as possible about other people and about things that are interesting. The third is that you get more joy out of giving joy to others and should put a good deal of thought into the happiness that you are able to give.

Eleanor Roosevelt

Be glad of life
because it gives
you the chance
to love and to work
and to play and to
look up at the stars.

Henry van Dyke

The grand essentials
to happiness
in this life are
something to do
something to love
and something
to hope for.

Joseph Addison

The Pursuit of Happiness

Happiness is an endowment and not an acquisition.
It depends more upon temperament and disposition
than environment. It is a state or condition of mind,
and not a commodity to be bought or sold in the
market. A beggar may be happier in his rags than a
king in his purple. Poverty is no more incompatible with
happiness than wealth, and the inquiry, "How to be
happy though poor?" implies a want of understanding
of the conditions upon which happiness depends.
Dives was not happy because he was a millionaire, nor
Lazarus wretched because he was a pauper. There is a
quality in the soul of man that is superior to
circumstances and that defies calamity and misfortune.
The man who is unhappy when he is poor would be
unhappy if he were rich, and he who is happy in a

palace in Paris would be happy in a dug-out on the frontier of Dakota. There are as many unhappy rich men as there are unhappy poor men. Every heart knows its own bitterness and its own joy. Not that wealth and what it brings is not desirable — books, travel, leisure, comfort, the best food and raiment, agreeable companionship — but all these do not necessarily bring happiness and may coexist with the deepest wretchedness, while adversity and penury, exile and privation are not incompatible with the loftiest exaltation of the soul.

 John J. Ingalls

The Pursuit of Happiness

Some of us might find happiness if we would
quit struggling so desperately for it.

William Feather

I accept life unconditionally....
Most people ask for happiness on condition.
Happiness can only be felt if you
don't set any condition.

Artur Rubinstein

Perfect happiness is the absence of the striving for happiness; perfect renown is the absence of concern for renown.

 Chuang-Tse

It was probably a mistake to pursue happiness; much better to create happiness; still better to create happiness for others. The more happiness you created for others the more would be yours — a solid satisfaction that no one could ever take away from you.

 Lloyd Douglas

☆ The Other Side of Happiness ☆

There are as many nights as days, and the one is just as long as the other in the year's course. Even a happy life cannot be without a measure of darkness, and the word "happiness" would lose its meaning if it were not balanced by sadness. It is far better to take things as they come along with patience and equanimity.

☆ Carl Gustav Jung

Happy the man
and happy he alone,
He who secure within
can say:
"Tomorrow doesn't
matter, for I have
lived today."

☆ Horace

In the midst of
winter, I finally
learned that there
was in me an
invincible summer.

☆ Albert Camus

⇒ Happiness Dwells Within ⇐

J oy is not in things; it is in us.

 Richard Wagner

V ery little is needed to make a happy life. It is all within yourself.

 Marcus Aurelius

Happiness
resides not in
possessions and
not in gold, the
feeling of happiness
dwells in the soul.

 Democritus

Happiness is not in our circumstances,
but in ourselves. It is not something we see,
like a rainbow, or feel, like the heat of a fire.
Happiness is something we are.

John B. Sheerin

⇒ *Happiness Is...* ⇐

...the calm, glad certainty of innocence.

 Henrik Ibsen

...the grace of being permitted to unfold... all the
spiritual powers planted within us.

 Franz Werfel

...the conviction that we are loved... in spite
of ourselves.

 Victor Hugo

...tranquility of mind.

Cicero

...enjoying the realities as well as the frivolities of life.

Edward G. Bulwer-Lytton

...made up of minute fractions... countless infinitesimals of pleasurable and genial feeling.

Samuel Taylor Coleridge

Happiness Is...

...the meaning and the purpose of life, the whole aim and end of human existence.

> Aristotle

...living on a farm which is one's own, far from the hectic, artificial conditions of the city — a farm where one gets directly from one's own soil what one needs to sustain life, with a garden in front and a healthy, normal family to contribute those small domestic joys.

> Thomas A. Edison

...a butterfly, which, when pursued,
is always just beyond your grasp,
but which, if you will sit down quietly,
may alight upon you.

 Nathaniel Hawthorne

...the quality of your thoughts.

Marcus Aurelius

Wish List

Of all the things I wish for you, I would give anything if these wishes could always come true...

I want you to be happy. I want you to fill your heart with feelings of wonder and to be full of courage and hope. I want you to have the type of friendship that is a treasure — and the kind of love that is beautiful forever. I wish you contentment: the sweet, quiet, inner kind that comes around and never goes away.

I want you to have hopes and have them all come true. I want you to make the most of this moment in time. I want you to have a real understanding of how unique and rare you truly are. I want to remind you that the sun may disappear for a while, but it never forgets to shine. I want you to have faith. May you have feelings that are shared from heart to heart, simple pleasures amidst this complex world, and wonderful goals that are within your grasp. May the words you listen to say the things you need to hear. And may a cheerful face lovingly look back at you when you happen to glance in your mirror.

I wish you the insight to see your inner and outer beauty. I wish you sweet dreams. I want you to have times when you feel like singing and dancing and laughing out loud. I want you to be able to make your good times better and your hard times easier to handle. I want you to have millions of moments when you find satisfaction in the things you do so wonderfully. And I wish I could find a way to tell you — in untold ways — how important you are to me.

Of all the things I'll be wishing for, wherever you are and whatever I may do, there will never be a day in my life when I won't be wishing for the best... for you.

 Collin McCarty

☆ Enjoy Yourself! ☆

If we are ever to enjoy life, now is the time.
Today should always be our most wonderful day.

☆ Thomas Dreier

I find ecstasy in living; the mere sense
of living is joy enough.

☆ Emily Dickinson

To live is not merely to breathe, it is to act;
it is to make use of our organs, senses,
faculties, of all those parts of ourselves
which give us the feeling of existence. The
man who has lived longest is not the man
who has counted most years, but he who
has enjoyed life most.

☆ Jean-Jacques Rousseau

Slow down and enjoy life. It's not only the scenery you miss by going too fast — you also miss the sense of where you're going and why.

 Eddie Cantor

Hold fast to dreams
for if dreams die,
life is a broken winged bird
that cannot fly.

 Langston Hughes

It is not how much we have, but how much we enjoy, that makes happiness.

 Charles H. Spurgeon

⊱ Work Toward Happiness ⊰

Who are the happiest people on earth?
A craftsman or artist whistling over a job well
done. A little child building sand castles.
A mother, after a busy day, bathing her baby.
A doctor who has finished a difficult and
dangerous operation, and saved a human life.
Happiness lies in a constructive job well done.

Get your happiness out of your work or you
will never know what happiness is.

 Elbert Hubbard

To be without desire is to be content. But contentment is not happiness. And in contentment there is no progress. Happiness is to desire something, to work for it, and to obtain at least a part of it. In the pursuit of beloved labor the busy days pass cheerfully employed, and the still nights in peaceful sleep. For labor born of desire is not drudgery, but manly play. Success brings hope, hope inspires fresh desire, and desire gives zest to life and joy to labor. This is true whether your days be spent in the palaces of the powerful or in some little green by-way of the world. Therefore, while yet you have the strength, cherish a desire to do some useful work in your little corner of the world, and have the steadfastness to labor. For this is the way to the happy life; with health and endearing ties, it is the way to the glorious life.

 Max Ehrmann

Work Toward Happiness

The Joy of Work

Give us, oh, give us, the man who sings at his work! He will do more in the same time — he will do it better — he will persevere longer. One is scarcely sensible of fatigue whilst he marches to music. The very stars are said to make harmony as they revolve in their spheres. Wondrous is the strength of cheerfulness, altogether past calculation in its powers of endurance. Efforts, to be permanently useful, must be uniformly joyous, a spirit all sunshine, graceful from very gladness, beautiful because bright.

— Thomas Carlyle

All real and wholesome enjoyments possible to man have been just as possible to him since first he was made of the earth as they are now; and they are possible to him chiefly in peace. To watch the corn grow, and the blossoms set; to draw hard breath over plowshare or spade; to read, to think, to love, to hope, to pray — these are the things that make men happy.

 John Ruskin

None but Freedom

Supreme happiness consists in self-content;
that we may gain this self-content, we are placed
upon this earth and endowed with freedom.

 Jean-Jacques Rousseau

The secret of Happiness is Freedom,
and the secret of Freedom, Courage.

 Thucydides

Our greatest happiness... does not depend
on the condition of life in which chance has
placed us, but is always the result of a
good conscience, good health, occupation,
and freedom in all just pursuits.

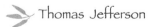 Thomas Jefferson

The necessity of pursuing true happiness is the foundation of our liberty.

 John Locke

Human happiness has no perfect security but freedom; freedom none but virtue; virtue none but knowledge.

 Josiah Quincy

Justice is the only worship. Love is the only priest. Ignorance is the only slavery. Happiness is the only good. The time to be happy is now. The place to be happy is here. The way to be happy is to make other people happy.

 Robert G. Ingersoll

Of Heart and Mind

Happiness itself is sufficient excuse. Beautiful things are right and true; so beautiful actions are those pleasing to the gods. Wise men have an inward sense of what is beautiful, and the highest wisdom is to trust this intuition and be guided by it. The answer to the last appeal of what is right lies within a man's own breast. Trust thyself.

 Aristotle

The happiest people are those who think the most interesting thoughts. Interesting thoughts can only live in cultivated minds. Those who decide to use leisure as a means of mental development, who love good music, good books, good pictures, good plays at the theater, good company, good conversation — what are they? They are the happiest people in the world; and they are not only happy in themselves, they are the cause of happiness in others.

 William Lyon Phelps

Of Heart and Mind

I have learned too much of the vanity of
human affairs to expect any felicity from
public life. But I am determined to be
cheerful and happy in whatever situation I
may be. For I have also learned from
experience that the greater part of our
happiness or misery depends on our
dispositions and not on our circumstances.

 — Martha Washington

A man's happiness and success in life will
depend not so much upon what he has, or
upon what position he occupies, as upon what
he is, and the heart he carries into his position.

S. J. Wilson

The more a man finds his sources of pleasure
in himself, the happier he will be....
The highest, most varied and lasting pleasures
are those of the mind.

Arthur Schopenhauer

A Union with God

The thought of God, and nothing short of it,
is the happiness of man.

Cardinal Newman

Happiness is neither within us only, nor
without us; it is the union of ourselves
with God.

 Blaise Pascal

Share with Others

All who joy would win
Must share it...
Happiness was born a twin.

 Lord Byron

Happiness is a sunbeam which may pass
through a thousand bosoms without losing a
particle of its original ray; nay, when it strikes
on a kindred heart, like the converged light
on a mirror, it reflects itself with redoubled
brightness. It is not perfected till it is shared.

Jane Porter

☆ Companions and Friends ☆

Much certainty of the happiness and purity of our lives depends on our making a wise choice of our companions and friends.

☆ John Lubbock

True happiness consists not in the multitude of friends, but in their worth and choice.

 Ben Jonson

The happiest moments my heart knows are those in which it is pouring forth its affections to a few esteemed characters.

Thomas Jefferson

Find Happiness
in Everything You Do

Find happiness in nature
in the beauty of a mountain
in the serenity of the sea
Find happiness in friendship
in the fun of doing things together
in the sharing and understanding
Find happiness in your family
in the stability of knowing
   that someone cares
in the strength of love and honesty
Find happiness in yourself
in your mind and body
in your values and achievements
Find happiness in
everything
you
do

 Susan Polis Schutz

ACKNOWLEDGMENTS

We gratefully acknowledge the permission granted by the following authors, publishers, and authors' representatives to reprint poems or excerpts from their publications.

Robert L. Bell for "Happiness" by Max Ehrmann. Copyright © 1948 by Bertha K. Ehrmann. All rights reserved. Reprinted by permission of Robert L. Bell, Melrose, MA, USA 02176.

Alfred A. Knopf, Inc. and Harold Ober Associates, Inc. for "Hold fast to dreams" from COLLECTED POEMS by Langston Hughes. Copyright © 1994 by the Estate of Langston Hughes. All rights reserved. Reprinted by permission.

For more information on Eddie Cantor, please contact the Eddie Cantor Appreciation Society, 14611 Valley Vista Boulevard, Sherman Oaks, CA 91403.

A careful effort has been made to trace the ownership of poems and excerpts used in this anthology in order to obtain permission to reprint copyrighted materials and give proper credit to the copyright owners. If any error or omission has occurred, it is completely inadvertent, and we would like to make corrections in future editions provided that written notification is made to the publisher:

BLUE MOUNTAIN PRESS, INC., P.O. Box 4549, Boulder, Colorado 80306.

May You Have Happiness

May your joys be as bright as the morning, and your sorrows merely be shadows that fade in the sunlight of love ∈ May you have enough happiness to keep you sweet ∈ Enough trials to keep you strong ∈ Enough sorrow to keep you human ∈ Enough hope to keep you happy ∈ Enough failure to keep you humble ∈ Enough success to keep you eager ∈ Enough friends to give you comfort ∈ Enough faith and courage in yourself to banish sadness ∈ Enough wealth to meet your needs ∈ And one thing more: Enough determination to make each day a more wonderful day than the one before.

An Irish Blessing